10.-

Apropos of Nothing

Books by Richard Jones

Country of Air
At Last We Enter Paradise
A Perfect Time
48 Questions
The Blessing
Apropos of Nothing

Apropos of Nothing

RICHARD JONES

COPPER CANYON PRESS

Printed in the United States of America

Cover art: Sung-Woo Chun (b. 1935), *The Nature Mandala, Number 9*, 1961. Oil on canvas, 63" x 45". Collection of the Whitney Museum of American Art, New York; Gift of John S. Bolles, A.I.A.   62.43

Copper Canyon Press is in residence at Fort Worden State Park in Port Townsend, Washington, under the auspices of Centrum Foundation. Centrum is a gathering place for artists and creative thinkers from around the world, students of all ages and backgrounds, and audiences seeking extraordinary cultural enrichment.

LIBRARY OF CONGRESS CATALOGING-IN-PUBLICATION DATA
Jones, Richard, 1953-
  Apropos of nothing / Richard Jones.
     p. cm.
  ISBN 1-55659-237-X (pbk. : alk. paper)
  I. Title.
  PS3560.O52475A86 2006
  811'.54—dc22

                                        2005028706

98765432   FIRST PRINTING

COPPER CANYON PRESS

Post Office Box 271
Port Townsend, Washington 98368
www.coppercanyonpress.org

Acknowledgments

The Comstock Review: "The Eye"

Crab Creek Review: "Ars Poetica"

Crying Sky: "Lorgnette," "The Lamps," "Freedom"

88: A Journal of Contemporary American Poetry: "The Sacrifice"

Great River Review: "The Messages," "The Spoon," "Home," "The Great Sky," "Philosophy of Life"

Image: "Immaculate," "The Obstacle"

The Literary Review: "Little"

The Louisville Review: "The Field Trip"

The Midwest Review: "The Rounds"

Onthebus: "Infinity and God," "The Rat," "The Balance," "Plums"

Poems & Plays: "The Diner"

Poetry International: "Sky Funeral"

Runes: A Review of Poetry: "Heft," "Always"

Smartish Pace: "The Sparrow," "Help," "Night"

South Dakota Review: "Things Not Seen"

The Southern Review: "The First Noble Truth"

Spillway Review: "The Other Side of the World," "The Day," "The Foot"

Timber Creek Review: "Cherries in the Snow"

Two Rivers Review: "I Like to Explore the Relationship between Myself and the Universe"

The epigraph is "The Beggary," by Cid Corman.

Contents

Of course, there is nothing to say,
and what I am saying is nothing.

But do you hear nothing?
Is this nothing?

Apropos of Nothing

Heft

I hold the words *broken bones*
in my hand; I hold the words
rib cage, the word *heart.*
I lift every word
like a stone or a feather.

The more beautiful words,
like *heaven,* or *nothingness,*
feel exactly the same
as *fence post* or *mailbox,*
lamplight or *shoelace.*

Spirit
flits like a tongue of flame,
as insubstantial in the hand
as its brother, *death,*
which weighs exactly the same as *life.*

The Messages

The answering machine clicks on,
offering messages
with none of the wisdom
I yearn to hear—
no voice announcing
strange revelations
into an ever-faithful tape,
no voice uttering sweet epiphanies
for me to replay
with the push of a button.
I would like to hear
a soliloquy
from Thomas Mann
on the religious fervor
of those laboring
on the edge of exhaustion—
fierce, obdurate German words
freighted with what it means
to renounce all sympathy
with the waiting abyss.
I'd appreciate
a few monosyllables
from Ernest Hemingway,
a dare to be kind
to the heart,
a brusque declaration
saying Do not
kill yourself,
a confidence telling me
he knows
how difficult it is
to write one true sentence.

I'd love Bashō
saying, "Listen
to the temple bell,
and when the bell stops,
to the sound coming out of the flowers...."

The First Noble Truth

My endodontist is a sly Buddha
teaching the noble truth of suffering.
He smiles at my fear, smiles at the way
I open my eyes to the searing light
or close them in search of soothing dark.

My doctor says, "Open wider ... wider,"
and kills me again and again with his needle.
His nurse addresses my soul, saying,
"It's not enough to endure
personal pain, private woe, suffering."

She tells me, "You'd have done better in life
to meditate on death, to sit by graves
and scrutinize the way of all flesh."
"Is it too late?" I ask, suffering,
fearing I've become Blake's sick rose,

but light floods my eyes, and the nurse,
like a dream, disappears. Now my doctor
illuminates the roots of suffering—
enlightening with drills and files,
attacking living nerve.

The doctor sees I'm plainly suffering,
asks how I am. "I'm burning away
to nothingness." "Good," he says,
"very good." Then he asks if there is pain.
"Yes," I say, "exquisite and clarifying."

Lorgnette

I'm going to ask my optometrist
for a lorgnette, a lorgnette
with slender black frames
and a graceful pearl handle.
I'm tired of heavy glasses
eternally pinching my nose.
Even when I've a new pair,
and leave the doctor's office
amazed by the clarity—
each green leaf visible
in the crown of the black locust—
it's only a matter of days before
I'm not seeing clearly at all,
needing never-ending adjustments
and lenses of different powers
for distance, foreground,
and reading. I read
like a nearsighted novitiate,
bending low,
close enough to kiss
the blue-gold page
of an illuminated manuscript.
But with a lorgnette,
I could donate my life's collection
to the Lions—
thick tortoiseshell,
horn-rimmed, and slim wire frames.
Done with glasses,
I'll be able to lift the lorgnette
to my face with intention and desire,
the holy desire to see,
to know

the world God made.
Yes, I'll visit the optometrist
and sit in the chair in the dark room
reading lines of small letters
projected on the wall.
The doctor will lean close
and swing before my face
the galaxy of his marvelous machine,
clicking lens after lens in front of two wide eyes,
asking,
Is this clear? Is this?

The Sparrow

I've been finding dead birds
in the grass in front of my house
and by the sidewalk on my way to work.
And I've begun to stop and pick them up,
a grackle, a jay, a starling,
holding them as if they were messengers,
as if they might speak.
On a busy corner some bright morning
you might find me standing still,
staring into my hand,
stroking the yellow wings of a finch.
I'm often tempted to slip the body into my coat—
feathers and wings in my pocket
all day as I teach
or follow my boys racing to the park.
Today, a sparrow in my palm
lay like the still silence
between the merest, the most trifling of thoughts.
I knelt by a tree and the sparrow fell from my fingers
like a gift not mine to carry, like the lightest of stones.

The Lamps

In our dark attic,
old lamps stand waiting
to be rewired, like neglected cars
in a field beside a repair shop,
awaiting their day
of resurrection.
Garnered from thrift stores
and purchased for almost nothing,
the lamps resemble monuments
in ornate graveyards—
a marble obelisk, a sleeping angel.
All have pull chains.
To turn on a light,
I have to genuflect
before a tasseled old shade,
bending low
to observe my thumb
and forefinger—
the tugging downward,
the letting go. It's easy
to forgive lamps
with chains that don't work—
I tilt my head,
listen for the *click,*
and just keep pulling,
as if turning the key
in the ignition of a car
that refuses to start.
For just as it's good
to motor down the highway
in a much-loved old car
with the window down,

the wind in your hair,
it's good
to retrieve old lamps from the attic
and return them to their purpose—
placed on tables
to flood the rooms with light.

I Like to Explore the Relationship between Myself and the Universe

In the high-ceilinged gallery
filled with elegant color-fields—
ravishing golds and eternal blues—
I fell in love with a painting's title.

The title's exuberance
and lack of modesty
included everything:
the barbs on the vane of a feather,
the hasp on a chest-lid,
gravity, lightning,
even ancient masters of poetry
in a moon-watching pavilion,
languidly lifting their sweeping silk sleeves
before inking brushes
to compose—

a woman hurrying over a bridge,
a river crane disappearing in mist,
the mountain road ascending into clouds.

Subwoofer

Beyond the green light, the road
circles the world like a line of poetry
that never runs out of breath
before coming round to this moment,

when a white Chevy Impala rolls to a stop,
subwoofer pulsing incessant sonic booms
that announce its kingdom and reign
over the intersection. On the corner,

waiting in line for the number 5 bus,
faces disgusted or uncomprehending turn
toward the driver, their stares rebuffed
by concentric circles of sound

that rattle shop windows, drown voices,
and echo inside the human chest
like a bully taunting our small
and very quiet hearts. Yet the driver—

shaved head, heavy-lidded eyes—
wears a face of serenity, like a monk
at one with the unremitting *Om*
of the universe in the locked trunk.

Tea Ceremony

I've set the microwave
to heat water for tea—
green tea with mint,
which, I confess, I take
with sugar and cream.
I know many consider
green tea with cream
and sugar uncivilized,
and that to prepare
tea so unceremoniously,
in a humming microwave,
forgoing ritual,
disparages grace and beauty.
But it's past midnight—
no one is watching.
And I am beginning
to understand
the unbearable
goodness of the hour—
tea, lightened by cream
and sweetened by sugar,
an occasion of eternity.
As I lean against the counter
with my arms crossed,
staring at the black
and white linoleum,
meditating on the desire
to refine my impoverishment,
embrace emptiness,
and rid myself
of the world's dust,
the microwave,

in the late-night
hush of my kitchen,
lucid and empty
as any evening bell,
tolls—calling me
to hot water for tea.

The Other Side of the World

lines composed in Xian, China

My new pencil notes
the way the beautiful
women of Xian
comport themselves—

their faces *masks of discretion,*
lean bodies *lonely as empty temples,*
their long straight hair—
natural as rain or moonlight.

And in the hollow
between their breasts—
silence—like a green jade necklace
hidden beneath a cotton dress.

Carrying neither handbag nor purse,
they walk empty-handed
and almost always
existentially alone

past American-style department stores
where battalions of clerks
in blue uniforms with yellow nametags
wait for someone

to ask a question
or buy a pencil,
as I did,
this morning.

I found myself
among the stationery goods
wishing to abandon
all languages

and simply hold the salesgirl's hand
as we stood
before scrolls of rice paper,
long-handled bamboo brushes, and black ink cakes.

Immaculate

When I heard God speaking in Spanish,
I turned and saw he was a young laborer
who'd come to wash the office windows.
He must have been working all morning—
small beads of sweat glistened on his brow—
and when he bowed to his bucket of soap,
I noticed his blue shirt, damp from the heat.
He worked quickly—his rag gushing a sudsy
blessing over the glass—and though the world
of my desk is but an arm's length from the window,
he never acknowledged me, but simply went
about his business, soaping the window vigorously,
then running his squeegee swiftly over the glass,
up and down, back and forth, the sign of the cross.

Infinity and God

My five-year-old is enamored of the words
infinity and *god,* employing them
to map space and time. God is bigger
than our house, bigger than the city, bigger
even than the biggest monster or spaceship.
A race car's *infinity fast,* boys eat *infinity cookies,*
his scrubbed face is, he says, *infinity shining—*
shining all the way up to God.

                    At day's end,
God shrinks—small enough to become
the perfect stillness and perfect silence
that rests at the end of his nightly prayer.
And infinity spirals down to a feather in his pillow.

Cherries in the Snow

My mother never appeared in public
without lipstick. If we were going out,
I'd have to wait by the door until
she painted her lips and turned
from the hallway mirror,
put on her gloves and picked up her purse,
opening the purse to see
if she'd remembered tissues.

After lunch in a restaurant
she might ask,
"Do I need lipstick?"
If I said yes,
she would discretely turn
and refresh her faded lips.
Opening the black and gold canister,
she'd peer in a round compact
as if she were looking into another world.
Then she'd touch her lips to a tissue.

Whenever I went searching
in her coat pocket or purse
for coins or candy
I'd find, crumpled,
those small white tissues
covered with bloodred kisses.
I'd slip them into my pocket,
along with the stones and feathers
I thought, back then, I'd keep.

The Spoon

Some days I think I need nothing
more in life than a spoon.
With a spoon I can eat oatmeal
or take the medicine doctors prescribe.
I can swat a fly sleeping on the sill
or pound the table to get attention.
I can point accusingly at God
or stab the empty air repeatedly.
Looking into the spoon's mirror,
I can study my small face in its shiny bowl,
or cover one eye to make half the world
disappear. With a spoon
I can dig a tunnel to freedom
spoonful by spoonful of dirt,
or waste life catching moonlight
and flinging it into the blackest night.

The Day

More and more now I do things alone—
lunch at the Roxy
with a book and coffee,
an afternoon matinee
at the Century.
Mine is a good town
to get lost in,
and I wander without care,
loitering in Bookman's Alley,
stopping in the antique shop
to ask the price of the Italian lamp
or the unsold Buddha
sitting in the window for months.
Like a solitary teenager skipping school
I can lean and loaf on library steps
and observe each passing face,
or dream under shade trees
in the cemetery,
my back against a stone seraph.
I walk
until mind and body drop away
and things themselves
are present to me—
book, lamp, Buddha, stone.
I'll spend all evening in the empty park
waiting on the first stars
and the moon,
but if it's time to go home,
I go home. Crossing the bridge—
a little tired, feet sore—
I imagine
the day after my death:

people calling on the crowded house
with offerings of flowers
and condolences,
someone off to the side
balancing a plastic plate of bean salad on her knees,
saying, "I used to see him downtown,
staring in shop windows in that peculiar way he had...."

Sky Funeral

In a revered Tibetan tradition,
I read aloud to my father,
the dead are borne to mountains
and the bodies offered to vultures.

I show him the photographs
of a monk raising an ax,
a corpse chopped into pieces,
a skull crushed with a large rock.

As one we contemplate the birds,
the charnel ground, the bone dust
thick as smoke flying in the wind.
Our dark meditation comforts us.

I ask if he'd like me to carry him—
like a bundle of sticks on my back—
up a mountain road to a high meadow
and feed him to the tireless vultures.

"Yes," he says, raising a crooked finger,
"and remember to wield the ax with love."

The Lieutenant

China, 1945

Peasants chase a man across a field,
beating him with sticks, corralling him
in a compound where animals are kept,
sheep and goats. My father said

the man was poor, wearing animal skins,
stinking of filth, that he was starving,
a homeless thief caught stealing food
from mountain people with little to eat.

The village had suffered an arctic winter.
My father said this is the way it was,
the way it had to be for them to endure.
The man is tied like an animal to a stake.

Screaming men take turns striking him,
taking his life with rods and pieces of pipe,
before the women and children punish
the dying body with scourging and curses.

"You going to do anything, Lieutenant?"
a sergeant asks. "No," he says, turning
from the compound, the bloodied thief.
"This has got nothing to do with us."

The Field Trip

visiting the Holocaust Museum
after reading Elie Wiesel's Night

I enter the empty freight car,
a box that carried many away.
Three girls and two boys—

I'd seen them in another gallery,
walking past the mounds of shoes—
board beside me, the two boys

pushing the giggling girls
up the ramp. In the quiet dark,
the teenagers huddle and whisper.

Their plan of escape is simple.
Tonight, past curfew, the girls
will elude their chaperones,

steal down the hotel hallway
to the boys' room, where, they say,
they'll order pizza and watch MTV.

No one says a word about kissing,
though that's all I thought about
when I was young. Even the boys

and girls herded onto the trains
flirted in the dark, or so I've read—
holding each other, gently rocking

as the wheels beneath them ground on.

The Rat

I lifted the farmhouse floorboards
to shine a flashlight, illuminating

twigs, paper, shredded plastic bags,
a sturdy nest

adorned with trinkets—
the broken nib of a fountain pen,

a silver bracelet laced
through a wall of straw and wire—

and black eyes
confronted by a spear of light

and apprehending the loss of their dark refuge
blazing and burning,

betraying full awareness—
instrument of destruction, annihilating hand.

The Balance

God guard me from those thoughts men think
                                    —YEATS

Intelligence is the savior
of emotion, for emotion on its own
is a storm of blades,
fields of broken glass....

And thought without emotion
is unredeemed, fact piled upon fact—
the number of beats in a line,
how many died in the conflagration....

But in the marrowbone
is the quest for truth
when men say there is no truth,
the struggle to discover meaning
in a universe men say has no meaning.
It is the way one learns to know, to love, to sing.

French Composition

I am late. A thousand pardons.
I wondered what had become of you.
I stopped at a barber's to be shaved and buy a cake of soap.
Let us sit down here at this table on the terrace.
Good. There is no wind and we will be very comfortable.
Waiter, a tea for my friend and a coffee for me.
What is going on in the square?
Lend me your field glasses. It is a puppet show.
Why do those people prefer the inside of the café?
They are busy writing letters or reading newspapers.
My mother and sister visited a pastry shop yesterday.
Dainty morsels do not fail to attract gentlemen
    as well as ladies.
I have spent two entire days at the Louvre.
You have done the essential thing.
Yes, but one soon gives up the idea of knowing all
    the schools of painting.
Does this make you cross?
Perhaps. It is sad to see the old regimes overthrown.
Do you think I should take my overcoat
    this evening?
You can relieve yourself of it in the cloakroom.
I understand if you tip the usher, he will
    look out for your interests.
In October I shall not be here anymore.
I shall not go to bed before your return.

Home

I spend a great deal of time
living in the past,
following Keats into the bower
where we meditate on the song of the nightingale,
or traveling with Goethe to Venice and Rome
to study art with Italian masters.
I like watching Beethoven at his desk,
the way deep creases appear on his brow
as he composes, or listening
to Bellini instruct the apprentice
who obediently mixes pigments
that become sacred, mystical light.
I relish nothing more than my long walks
with Wordsworth, or my cup of tea
with Dickens, except, perhaps, sailing
with Shelley to doom's horizon,
or hearing Laurence Sterne
reading aloud from Ovid's *Art of Love.*
How lucky I am to sit all day on the hill,
looking out upon the infinite with Leopardi,
who, like me, accepts that he is nothing,
or to wend my way home through tortured streets
at midnight with Dante Alighieri,
stealing past the prostitute illumined by the moon.

The Diner

The short-order cook and the dishwasher
argue the relative merits
of Rilke's *Elegies*
against Eliot's *Four Quartets,*
but the delivery man who brings eggs
suggests they have forgotten *Les fleurs
du mal* and Baudelaire. The waitress
carrying three plates and a coffeepot
can't decide whom she loves more—
Rimbaud or Verlaine,
William Blake or William Wordsworth.
She refills the rabbi's cup
(he's reading Rumi),
asks what he thinks of Arthur Waley.
In the booth behind them, a fat woman
feeds a small white poodle in her lap,
with whom she shares her spoon.
"It's Rexroth's translations of the Japanese,"
she says, "that one can't live without:
*May those who are born after me
Never travel such roads of love.*"
The revolving door proffers
a stranger in a long black coat,
lost in the madhouse poems of John Clare.
As he waits to be seated,
the woman who owns the place
hands him a menu
in which he finds several handwritten poems
by Hāfez, Gibran, and Rabindranath Tagore.
The lunch hour's crowded—
the owner wonders
if the stranger might share
my table. As he sits,

I put a finger to my lips,
and with my eyes ask him
to listen with me
to the young boy and the young girl
two tables away
taking turns reading aloud
the love poems of Pablo Neruda.

The Eye

Grief gets her up in the morning,
and death, a little boy,
takes her by the hand
and leads her through town—
the roadside littered
with broken-down cars, rusting
old stoves, twisted shopping carts,
the houses shuttered, abandoned,
things in dark shops heavy with dust.
From cracked windows in gray tenements,
ashen faces without affect
behold the pair
walking the filthy streets.
When they come to the schoolhouse—
a boy with his book bag, a woman
with her worn leather satchel and glasses—
death sits in the front row. A bright pupil,
he opens a blank notebook, finds his pen.
When he is ready she takes chalk,
writes the thought for the day on the blackboard,
a bit of advice from Wordsworth, "Beware
the tyranny of the eye." Then she hears
the little boy repeating to himself,
beware, beware, the tyranny, the eye.

The Answer

Tonight, looking for the answer,
I must have killed an hour
flipping through philosophy and poetry books,
every few minutes opening and reading a different title.
I anxiously searched all the places I keep books—
looking in the kitchen, the boys' rooms,
checking the laundry room and workshop,
before going outside finally to the curb
to search through books tossed
in the backseat of the car.
Snow fell straight down in windless silence.
The keys in my left hand jingled like very small bells.
I stopped and tried to remember
what I'd come into the night looking for.

The Foot

I wanted to give something back
to the world—
all the light-painted meadows,
the vast ceiling of stars above the deserts,
the blind cliffs rising up from the sea.
I decided to plant a seventy-nine-cent
three-inch pot of blue petunias
in a long-neglected corner of the garden.
Singing a little song, I knelt down,
and pushed the trowel into the dirt.
Just below the surface, I hit something hard—
a bit of white marble. The next moment
I unearthed the strong ankle and shapely foot
of a young athlete, a god, a shepherd boy.
Or perhaps it was a maiden's ankle, I thought
as I washed the marble fragment under the hose.
Even a virgin's foot, were it made of stone,
would be heavy, I reasoned,
and to the potting shed I carried the treasure
to buff with a wire brush
between its toes.

Plums

I liken death to a bowl
of ripe purple plums
enjoyed on the terrace
of a high mountain lodge
at dawn above a quiet lake,
the water touched with light,
spruces on the eastern slopes
still deep in purple shadow
the color of the wine-dark flesh
of plums so startlingly sweet
one quickly devours the fruit
down to the hard, pocked,
living stone of the pit.

The Ruin

I've made a garden path
from broken bricks
and paving stones
winding among
daylilies and daisies,
past bee balm and peonies,
and coming to an end
among feverfew,
meadow sage,
and switchgrass,
a path with nothing
of the sublime,
nothing
of the mystery of nature,
though at journey's end
I have begun
to arrange a ruin—
fragments of marble columns,
shattered statuary,
cracked stone tablets
and wooden crosses—
wreckage of the world
I leave for moss and lichen.

Help

At night, when I help my father
up the stairs, we take each step slowly,
my steady hand on the small of his back.

In his room, I hover with a tiny bottle
of eyedrops. *Open, open,* I say.
His tears catch the lamplight, and shine.

As I cover him with an extra blanket,
and bend to kiss him good night, he lies
still, thin arms crossed over his chest,

face as peaceful as an alabaster mask.
Each night, when I turn out the light,
I stand in the dark. Soon my father's life

will be motes of dust drifting in light,
and his spirit will be as a piece of thread
slipping easily through the eye of a needle.

Always

a baby
        crying in the next room,
                a wineglass
falling from a table,
        a knife sharpened,
                a splinter in the eye,
a broken wing,
        a ruined cistern,
                the false witness,
an empty vase
        in an empty room,
                dried, dead flies on a sill,
a ditch
        and a horse cart
                with shattered wheels,
a sinking boat,
        burning violins,
                vultures
huddled over a corpse,
        the ax
                at the foot of the tree.

The Sacrifice

Søren Kierkegaard says to suffer
more precisely. Let the bitter soul be
loved by God.

Does he know what he's asking?
When a man has lived even a few years,
the heart's a grave, a poor burial plot. Look—

there they lie buried in forgetfulness:
promises, intentions, resolutions,
not to mention the shadows of crimes and lies.

Still, Kierkegaard insists on surrender:
empty the self in tranquil abandon.

He uses words like *unchangeableness*
or *fear and trembling*. He quotes Scripture—
purity of heart is to will one thing.

Be love's sacrifice.
Sacrifice, Kierkegaard would insist.

Kierkegaard sounds like God, who asks,
"Have you now anything to complain of?
Though embittered by childhood and youth,
do you not now have my infinite love?"

Blind Milton Dictating to His Daughters

after the painting by Fuseli

The two daughters
have agreed to turns at the lectern,
writing down
on a white tablet
what their father says,
though the girl at work—
leaning on an elbow,
daydreaming,
unaware of the divine
light exalting the white page
and lending her a resplendent glow—
seems not terribly interested
in explaining the ways of man
to God. In red velvet slippers
and flowing, blue-white gown,
she's simply an obedient daughter
setting down line after
perfect line. Meanwhile,
in the room's shadows
the other daughter,
unheeded by her father,
waits. Primly seated on a low stool,
she sews a length of thin white fabric—
a shawl, or perhaps a petticoat.

The Great Sky

One may write of nothing
but the blue heron, solitary, elegant,
thin as a reed rising from the marsh,

the owl, deliberating in a tree
at midnight, the white face, the black eyes,
the furred ears tuned to the forest's faintest *snap,*

the crow attending to the dead
dragonfly's empty husk,
wind-shuddered wings still shimmering,

the hawk circling, spying
a rabbit in the rushes bowing
under the weight of the sky,

the house sparrow's nest of twigs
under the eaves of the garden shed,
the clutch of yellow eggs ready to hatch.

Freedom

In Shanghai—
above the tangle of alleys
between the Dragon Wall
and Jade Buddha Temple—
I'll rent a modest flat
that offers unhindered views
of the junks and ferries
on the crowded Yangtze.
I'll paint my rooms black—
they will shine peacefully
like the river in moonlight.
When guests arrive with flowers
I'll attend them politely,
then rise and show them out.
Alone at a table inlaid with ivory,
the air blue with incense,
I'll unroll scrolls to contemplate.
I'll pace before the window
carrying a fly whisk,
flicking away buzzing memories—
faces, towns, sorrow, happiness.
In black silk pajamas and slippers,
I'll spend nights meditating
on the heart's longing
to know the unknowable.
And if I never cross the world,
if I never get to Shanghai
and find the peaceful room shining
like black water above the Dragon Wall,
I'll build—
beneath my left rib cage—
a city of narrow streets,

river barges, and smokestacks.
Beijing, the northern capital,
will be my right elbow,
and the tips of my ears,
the high mountains guarding the Shaolin Temple.

The Caravan

For once I'm up before the sun, alone
in the empty and peaceful kitchen,
pouring coffee and cream,
anticipating an agreeable morning
uninterrupted at the desk,
followed by an afternoon with books
and long, quiet evening hours,
when I hear horses and ringing bells,
an old man's voice, singing.
I hesitate, a spoonful of sugar hovering
above the cup, and listen a moment,
then walk to the picture window
to behold the spectacle—
a caravan coming down the lane.
Six painted wagons in a row
circle between the boxwood hedges
and the blossoming roses, and halt,
the wagons only feet from the window.
One of the draft horses, a white star
on its brow, swivels its great head,
blinking, snorting, twitching its left ear,
and thoughtfully considers my face
while it waits to be free of bridle and bit.

Small fires burn on the lawn,
blue smoke rising in the gray light
as boys water the horses
and a man with flashing knives
leads a tethered goat away
to be slaughtered for supper.
As the sun brings the day into being,
women, yawning and stretching,

emerge through narrow wagon doors,
lifting their long, flowing skirts
to step barefoot down two steps,
where behind the caravan they
leisurely unbutton frilly blouses
and bathe with frayed silk scarves
dipped in barrels of cool rainwater.
The men stand about drinking
black coffee from dented tin cups.
From the shade of the box elder,
their leader appears, zipping his fly,
a graying, hatless, sturdy old man
in threadbare pants and worn boots.
He takes stock of his troupe, weary
from their journey, hunkered down,
smoking pipes or sleeping in the shade
under the wagons, heads on their coats.
Then he takes a black waistcoat
from atop the hedge where he left it,
shrugs it on, brushes away a leaf,
looks at the sky, approaches my door
and knocks, one thunderous blow.

I clear papers and thick volumes
from the long table where I work.
I ask if he'd eat; he requires nothing.
The two of us sit. His black eyes
survey shelves heavy with books;
for a long moment he is silent,
as if waiting for me to speak.
At last I confess a fear of reading.
Reading makes me nervous—
mortal—I say, and I dislike feeling
mortal, thinking of my sour bones

moldering in the grave
like those of the long-dead poets.
The old man listens quietly.
I say now that I've grown old,
long-concealed desires have ripened.
I fall from one confusion to the other,
find the freedom I once loved meaningless.
Never before have I, a poet, wished
to renounce language,
but, I say, I will.
I'll abandon speech, conversation,
even poems,
no longer having anything to say.

The old man asks if he might bother me
for a glass of water, which he drinks
in one long, loud gulp. He wants to know
what I think of the world, what I want
from life—if I have lived, here on earth,
like a man, the life to which I was called.
I say I regret I did not begin earlier
to train my eye and search for wisdom.
If I had lived as a monk,
praying in my cell in a stone monastery
high on a mountaintop,
if I'd gazed at the same sky and stars
from the same window each day
for fifty years, perhaps I'd have found
a symbol—a tree, or a bend in the river
far below in the valley,
great white clouds drifting by—
to clarify that which I was seeking.
I dismiss my comments
with a wave of a hand in the air,

admit all my endeavors have been nothing.
And still, I say, the search for wisdom
requires everything. *Wisdom,* I say, *and mercy.*

The old man shakes his head *no,*
and tells me I have forgotten
the main thing, the greatest virtue,
but says no more. Instead, he rises,
fetches a bottle of wine from the sideboard.
I bring bread, which he tears in two
and eats dispassionately. We drink,
lifting our glasses in a silent toast.
The old man leans across the table,
takes my hand in his scarred, leathery hand.
He tells me that in the bed in the black wagon
that travels from one strange place to another,
his wife lies dying. Her gray hair
hangs to her waist at night—
black as a river, once.
She was a child when they wed;
his torment has been
to witness time and time's power,
and soon, tomorrow, perhaps,
he will bury her.
He nods his head *true, true,* but then
he smiles, and I see he wishes to comfort me.
And now, he says, releasing my hand
and filling my glass, tell me
what you have failed to mention,
tell me about the greatest thing,
the main virtue,
love.

Darkness falls and deepens.
Stars enrich the sky
and a new moon hangs over the caravan.
In bed, I drift,
listening to guitars and violins,
imagining lamplit lovers in the wagons,
their damp, narrow beds,
the black pillows.
I close my eyes to see
the old man
reading aloud by a candle,
sitting up late beside
his sleepless wife.
Before the light comes,
I wake to bells
as the caravan takes to the path
that goes on forever
and never ends,
wooden wheels turning, the slow
hoofbeats pounding moments in time.
As the world turns and the night slowly dies,
I rise from my pillow, open
my eyes, and then, as the caravan
takes to the open road,
I hear the old man,
singing.

Saved

between the pages
of a handbook on prosody—
monarch wings

Eternity or What

I. The Rounds

After a long hard day doing nothing,
I turn in early
while there's still some blue
painting the window.
I like to lie in bed
surrounded by pillows and quiet,
slowly turning the pages of a novel.
With a cup of strong tea,
I'll gladly go anywhere
the words care to take me,
though sometimes it's good to drowse,
book open on my chest
like two comforting hands.
There's joy
lying in the dark at the center of things,
trying to see,
and seeing little,
a lesson in the way things are.
All night
that's what the crickets chatter about.
Poor crickets—
no bed or cup of tea,
no novel to read until morning.
A cricket might lie
in bed forever,
but I get up,
put on a robe,
walk through the neighborhood.
I shuffle in slippers,

murmuring blessings
upon shadowed doors and black windows.
It makes little difference
if God is listening
or busy with dawn on the other side of the world;
what matters
is that at the end of my rounds,
back at the border between waking and dreams,
my bed and book are waiting.

II. The Musician

On a blue sofa by the window, I lie listening
to thunder, or the cry of a bird, or—in the hush
of falling snow—sweet, unimpeachable silence.

With each day I, too, am lifted up, a rare violin
taken from its locked leather case and played.

III. Night

Each night I worked
at the cluttered desk,
the lake below the window
shining in moonlight,
spiraling cedars casting long,
immaculate shadows
in the white meadow.
Near sunrise I'd go
downstairs, out the back door
to wander—blue fog-clouds
afloat over hay fields
and streams, the mountains
one long blue brushstroke.
Sometimes I'd walk
through nearby woods,
the moldering earth
as sweet to me as the oaks,
ferns, wild rhododendron,
and sometimes I'd leave
my clothes on the bank,
wade through the shallows,
and swim through black water.
And sometimes I'd stay
near the house, looking up
at the study's dark window.
In the simple quiet under the pines,
I'd think about bed
and resting a little, eyes closing
while bright veils settled
everywhere. Sometimes
I'd drift down the dirt lane
to welcome the day,
looking back once or twice to see

the porch in blue-green shadow,
the gables glowing white.
At lane's end I'd turn, walk back
to sleep in the growing light,
waking in the late afternoon
alone on a tattered gold sofa,
the mind uncluttered, shining,
like the moon, waiting to rise.

IV. Things Not Seen

Sitting at my desk
watching the sky,
I saw the hawk
swoop down
from a loblolly pine
on the hillock
toward the house.
The rust-colored
pinion feathers—
swept back, slicing
the heavy summer air—
loomed large
in the window.
I could even see
flecks of gold
in the all-seeing eye
that spies,
from its mountain perch,
dim-sighted voles
digging in the meadow.

The window shattered
and the hawk
lay still on the floor
among pieces of glass
as sharp as any knife-edge.
I went downstairs
to find broom and dustpan.
At the pantry mirror,
I noted I was bleeding
under my left eye.
When I returned,
the hawk had risen
and, leaving not a feather behind,
had found the open window.

I wrote in the room
as I had all year,
the broken
window covered with cardboard and tape
until the days began getting shorter,
darker, and I could feel winter coming.
The replacement glass I cut, caulked,
and set into the wooden frame
was too clear—
different from the wavy
opalescent glass
in every other century-old
window of the rambling farmhouse.

All winter and spring
at my desk, I struggled
to write about the hawk.
What could I say
to make anyone believe?
All the proof is gone—
the broken glass
long since thrown out
and ground underfoot,
the cardboard pane, burned as kindling,
now, with the woodstove cinders,
returned to the garden's earth.

And I never again saw
the hawk gliding
over the fields and hills.
Even the scar, here, under my left eye,
is gone.

v. Little

This morning we did everything—
built turreted castles from cardboard boxes,
swam like sharks in the plastic pool,
talked in monotones like alien robots.
With sidewalk chalk we drew angels—
blue wings, red helmets, silver lances—
and named them Gabriel and Michael.
At noon I showed Sarah a starling.
I tilted yellow tulips to spill the cool
of rainwater into William's cupped hands.
We upturned the garden's rocks
and kneeled to scrutinize new life writhing—
grubs and nymphs twirling in the sensual dirt.
Then Andrew raised a sword of light—
the enemy army attacked and we fought
to the death like ninja; the battle won,
we rose, surveyed the wreckage, gave thanks,
and wiped men's blood from our brows.
Later we walked to the sunset-sea and made salt.
At twilight, atop our royal elephants, we slowly
crossed the Himalayas. At evening's threshold,
we sat on the back porch and marveled
at the way an ankle bends, a hand opens.
Night came on. We charted Orion's progress
in the sky. Then we nestled like deer in tall grass.
The warm dark concealed us and I felt *happy*,
having accomplished little all day.

Ars Poetica

When I think of writing poems
I get lonely and think of my dog,
her last days on earth
when she shivered and trembled.
When she was young she loved to swim.
Summer mornings, before the heat came,
I'd stand with my mug of coffee
and throw the stick
far out into the black water of the lake,
and she'd heave her big black body
after it in desperation, always bringing
it back, the stick, the love. All night
she'd lay beneath my desk, sleeping
as I wrote, lightning flashing
in the storm of the mind. I remember
when she was so small I could hold her
in one hand as I worked,
how I learned to type with one finger—
all I needed to write.

Philosophy of Life

I'm at home on a train
trundling down an icy mountain,
or on a midnight ferry
crossing some storm-tossed strait,
or in the backseat of a taxi at twilight,
looking out the window at streetlamps,
silent stone bridges and black water.
Rucksack on my back, I'm happy
to linger in the station studying timetables
or to mingle with crowds on village streets
before wandering into the country,
out to the blossoming orchards and fields.
When night falls, I'm sitting quietly
on a hillside, listening to distant bells,
at home with the silence that answers
my questions. But if I'm lucky,
I find an open barn, take a pitchfork
and fashion a bed of fresh straw. Then
I'll lie all night, listening to my companions,
the cows, discussing their philosophy of life.

The Obstacle

I was in the garden, reading Brother Lawrence. It was early, the sun slanting through the neighbor's birches. I was reading his letters under the table umbrella, drinking coffee, half listening to birdsong, half studying the light falling on the grass. I was in the garden in the backyard, contemplating eternity, looking at the grass, and thinking how dark, almost black, the grass seemed in the umbrella's shadow. I was reading Brother Lawrence—not reading so much as reciting one or two lines at random, chanting as if in prayer. I was trying to focus; the grass was dark, almost black. I looked around the garden for God to worship in his presence, as Brother Lawrence did in France in the monastery four hundred years ago. I put the book down and stopped praying—Brother Lawrence warned that even prayer could take one away from God.

About the Author

Richard Jones was born in London, reared in Virginia, and is currently professor of English at DePaul University in Chicago. He is the author of five previous books of poetry, most recently *The Blessing: New and Selected Poems*. He lives north of the city with his wife, Laura, and their children, Sarah, William, and Andrew.

The Chinese character for poetry is made up of two parts: "word" and "temple." It also serves as pressmark for Copper Canyon Press.

Founded in 1972, Copper Canyon Press remains dedicated to publishing poetry exclusively, from Nobel laureates to new and emerging authors. The Press thrives with the generous patronage of readers, writers, booksellers, librarians, teachers, students, and funders — everyone who shares the conviction that poetry invigorates the language and sharpens our appreciation of the world.

Major funding has been provided by:

Anonymous
The Paul G. Allen Family Foundation
Lannan Foundation
National Endowment for the Arts
Washington State Arts Commission

Copper Canyon Press gratefully
acknowledges Madeleine Wilde,
whose generous Annual Fund support
made publication of this book possible.

For information and catalogs:

COPPER CANYON PRESS
Post Office Box 271
Port Townsend, Washington 98368
360-385-4925
www.coppercanyonpress.org